Rhyme & Refrain

Rhyme & Refrain

David Jalajel

UNIVERSITY *of the* WESTERN CAPE

UNIVERITY *of the* **WESTERN CAPE**

Copyright © 2017 David Jalajel
2019 re-issue

Published by the University of the Western Cape
Department of Foreign Languages
Private Bag X17, Bellville 7535
Western Cape, South Africa

All rights reserved. No part of this publication may be reproduced, stored in a retrieval system, or transmitted, in any form or any means, electronic, mechanical, photocopying, recording, or otherwise, without prior permission of the author or the University of the Western Cape.

ISBN 978-0-86808-764-1

All of the works in this collection have previously appeared in *The Ghazal Page: The International Journal of English Language Ghazals*.

Cover illustration: a detail from Fortunato Depero's "Guerra-festa", 1925. National Gallery of Modern Art, Rome.

Dedicated to:

GENE DOTY

*a great champion of the ghazal in English,
a fine poet, and a dear friend.*

Contents

After Persian Ghazals are Explained to an Arab Poetaster	9
Joseph	10
Basilosaurus	11
The Tinkerer	12
The Tinkerer's Workshop	13
Noah – an oratorio	14
The Goal	18
Convalescence	19
Ghazal for the Ghoul Maiden	20
A17g	21
A60g2	22
A70g	23
A76g	24
A89g	25
A97g	26
The Lovely Ghoul	27
The Cave	28
Sa(l)vaging the Starlet	29
Stone Tenses	30
Volcán de Fuego	31
Essay: A Short History of the Ghazal	33

After Persian Ghazals are Explained to an Arab Poetaster

Your explanation's just one long, defeated word.
No verse can bear the weight of a repeated word.

A truth is never humble when enshrined in verse
But will not stand to rival a conceited word.

I'd fail to kiss the beauty of her parting lips
Since she is bound to utter such a cheated word.

A sage advises his disciples clear their eyes,
And I suggest you ponder a deleted word.

Each house must bake and butter its own wholesome bread.
How can you honour guests with that preheated word?

I'll wish to watch the feature playing on the screen
And not the tiresome head of that reseated word.

Yes, the stool pigeon cries with mournful eyes of love –
Until it splatters your hat with that excreted word.

My father's father sold you several cups of tea
So you can drink down easily that meat-head word!

Joseph

"I know, my son, your starry vision. Below that sky there's the wolf.
I fear that in their feral envy you will die for the wolf."

"Please, O Father, we will keep him with us at all times."
He let him go, for now his ghostly heart grew shy of the wolf.

In the darkness of the well they heard the water splash,
But then the pit breathed in, and the dusky spring fell dry for the wolf.

"It augurs evil to tell an open lie to a ghostly man,
But let our bloody gestures and our tongues imply it's the wolf."

They came before him holding a child's torn and bloodied shirt:
"Father! 'He is our youngest brother' we did cry to the wolf."

Though she was cunning, and her heat fired the passion of a king,
He was resolved within his soul he would not lie with the wolf.

"In this cell your dreams foretell my station on the Earth.
Seven years of drought will end upon the sigh of the wolf."

"Bring your ghostly father, so he may see who wields the staff."
Inside he smiled and was sated. His thoughts were wry towards the wolf.

The father's tears were wiped now with a grown man's musky shirt.
He beheld his son, King David's father, with the keen eye of the wolf.

Basilosaurus

Saharan whales from under the ground
Are runes telling tales from under the ground.

Shorn bones arch up like sculpted dunes
Or giant sea snails from under the ground.

Fins, ribs and jaws entreat the sky
Like ivory sails from under the ground.

Breaking the sand, white serpents writhe
And flick up their tails from under the ground.

Throughout the night, these dry tongues lick
At salt-crusted shales from under the ground.

Each bleary dawn, bleached voices call
A face that unveils from under the ground.

The seas they'd ploughed with monstrous grace
Now pound out fierce gales from under the ground.

The Tinkerer

Tinker around. Forge your contrived matter. Hammer in time.
In spiralling thoughts, work & shape your plans faster in time.

Work them on your inexplicable lathe, in realms where our
Lucid souls can't, in our haziest dreams, venture in time.

From metals & ores, base & untempered, contrive gears,
Cogs & springs, a legion of machines to muster in time.

Machines with designed idiosyncrasies, fated to malfunction:
Like circuitry that flashes, sparks, & spurts fire in time...

& sensitive light sensors, their cables ahead of them,
Their sight blocked by each swing of snarled wire in time...

A gear sawed in half & affixed to a cylinder, a makeshift thumb
Pivoting, pinching & releasing a clawed grasper in time.

They work & they fail, breaking down constantly, sputtering,
Colliding in frail crashes, glass cascades that shatter in time.

Yours is a chaotic hodgepodge of inventiveness frolicking
In faltering motions – yet they dance all together in time.

The Tinkerer's Workshop

It's a quaint cubical structure, a brick boxlike affair,
Yet it stands graceful, composed, like a sculpture now

Of function, elegance & taste. It's a sublime edifice
That's nearly perfect – but there's a fissure in one corner now.

Just a gap of one brick, neatly removed from its place,
But perfection is eluded. It's a wounded structure now.

The people converge, gathering round the workshop, weeping.
How they puzzle & moan, groping for an answer now.

They circle the walls incessantly. But over & again
Their eyes befall the maiming gap. Their hearts grow madder now.

They cry & wail: "O! if that brick were just there." & they start
To doubt the sense, & wisdom, of the one who tinkers now.

So what happens, as the tinkerer emerges & replaces the brick
In the gap? How do they bear the unsought closure now?

Noah – an oratorio

Chorus of angels:

> "Fear God's presence, clouds and rain,
> His ever-present clouds and rain."

Chorus of priests:

> "Bring the harvest, give us grain,
> O, acquiescent clouds and rain."

Noah:

> "How they call false gods in vain,
> Craving to hasten clouds and rain."

Chorus of priests:

> "Full-moon harvest, gibbous grain,
> We summon crescent, clouds, and rain."

Noah:

> "Don't pray to gods who wax and wane,
> Invoking pagan clouds and rain."

Chorus of priests:

> "This stone altar blood must stain.
> Appease the trenchant clouds and rain."

Noah:

> "I implore you, fear the bane
> Of bloated, tumescent clouds and rain."

Chorus of priests:

> "To our gods our voices strain:
> Hear us, sentient clouds and rain!"

Noah:

> "Heed my warning, son, again
> Of unrepentant clouds and rain."

Noah's son:

> "Shall I fear a weathervane,
> Evanescent clouds, and rain?"

Chorus of people (a):

    "Erupting from stones! Engulfing the plain!
    What effervescent clouds and rain!"

Chorus of people (b):

    "Flee from your homes! Flee from the plain!
    From coalescent clouds and rain!"

Noah:

    "Ship's timbers stretch. The beasts complain:
    Oh, omnipresent clouds and rain!"

Chorus of angels:

    "Forty nights will rise and wane
    Through fierce, incessant clouds and rain."

Noah:

    "Seek the coastline. Hark! The main –
    Iridescent clouds and rain."

Noah:

> "The beauty of the Earth regained:
> Soft and pleasant clouds and rain."

Chorus of angels:

> "All life on Earth shall be sustained
> By God's benevolent clouds and rain."

Chorus of people:

> "Tree and flower... Fox and crane...
> Deer and pheasant. Clouds and rain."

The Goal

She is prepared to split your life asunder for the goal.
Her lawyer's reputation might go under for the goal.

His wish to count the stars consumes his thoughts, yet his desires
Surrender to his blinding sense of wonder for the goal.

Don't think your bankroll's steep enough to keep you high and dry.
It's not enough to merely be a funder for the goal.

Longships scour the coasts we'd scorched with prayers and steeped in stones,
Axes, swords and spears invoking plunder for the goal.

The campaign trail is lonely, but the brass band plays in time
With royal pomp and presidential thunder for the goal.

The storm clouds paint the field with shades of wet and shades of clay
In which our nation's players blindly blunder for the goal.

Convalescence

Your clinical numbness is cognitive dissonance,
So you cop a good mood swing, nursing your doubts again.

You implicate, meekly, the staff in your feelings,
But they switch off their pagers, rushing about again.

They scribble requests on the board by the chapel.
The doctors want coffee cups – but you turn devout again.

The tile on the floor here is like your old icebox.
Won't they open a window & let the air out again?

Your footfalls are firm for one skirting old age – now,
Press on down the passage & shake off your gout again.

Ghazal for the Ghoul Maiden

These ravens I summon drink blood from the barn owls
that nest at my feet. How my passion affrights her.

She hears the death cries of my nestlings & cringes,
but her birth here inside this dry valley excites her.

The frost of her spirit congeals on my toenails
& burns like the sunset as twilight ignites her.

Now I read, from the archives anonymous queens &
viziers have sequestered, a parchment that cites her.

It summons her fortunes, unfetters her glory,
& foretells how cold creatures did scrape, claw & bite her.

The stress of her waking bears down on my ankles
while the darkness encircles the moonglow that lights her.

A weakness of breathing comes after the darkness
when her body is bared & the years come to blight her.

I'll insist she climbs up to the sky's humble vision
until heaven is willing to step down & right her.

When her new voice turns white, when her blue eyes turn yellow,
it's time for the moon to come out & delight her.

She's all that the soul can embrace beyond dying,
& it's all for her love that I dare to requite her.

A17g

A60g2

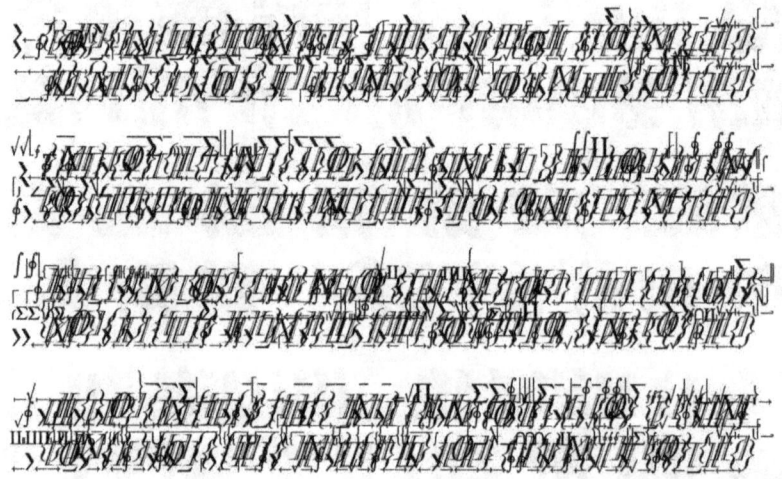

A70g

A76g

A89g

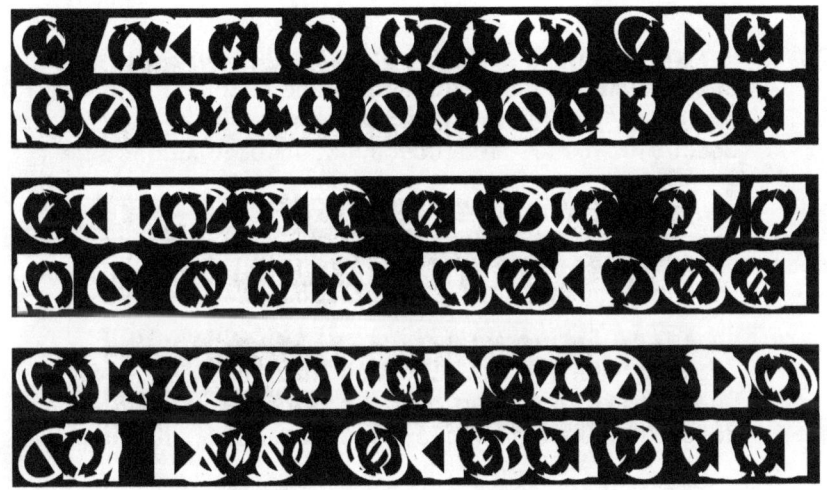

A97g

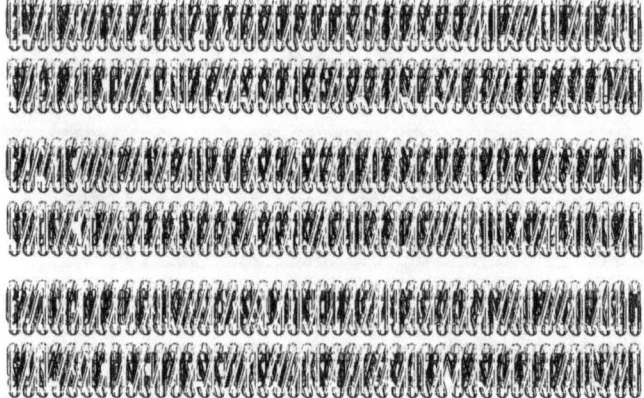

The Lovely Ghoul

Her hair flying like a flock of ravens
Shocked by ravens,

She mocks the ravens –
Nesting in the clock with ravens

Unlocked by ravens.
No gulls perch on the dock. They're ravens.

The unmistakable knock of ravens
Hewn into each hill and each rock by ravens.

The Cave

Phantom forms flicker and dance at the fore of the cave.
What care prisoners for Plato's ghosts? The ground is damp.
The dogs are real. Their sharp pain is sure of the cave.

Embrace the anointment – its Nero's Rome. The cavern's call
Comes to the sleepers on a seraph's decree. A feral son
Stands guard like the dour Moon at the door of the cave.

The call to read comes from a voice with kaleidoscope wings.
Wild fear flutters in a confusion of visions and signs.
Voices rise with the awe of language and the lore of the cave.

A spider dances on signs of emptiness. The seekers read
Writings on silk and turn away. Untold words
Waken the air – with a final sigh – on the floor of the cave.

Sa(l)vaging the Starlet

Her stumble's nebulous, so they start to question
the image her body projects. Superstitious actors
from the guild will toil and trouble on opening night.

So do a little digging. She's iridescent, irresistible,
and you'll uncover all the covetous estates when
the paparazzi begin to grumble on opening night.

They curse her – conjuring up a cocoon of lust. So
her evolution becomes a supernatural notion: one
that promises to bare her stubble on opening night.

Engage her surroundings. It'll all be press-worthy (yet
elusive) after the franchise bursts its bubble – and then
the tinsel islands will start to tumble on opening night.

Shaped by sports machines: a young star who'd struggled
with her lyrics – Now she's red-hot, a comet on the Hill,
and she's ripe to show she's supple on opening night.

Stone Tenses

The temple drips, like water through torn stone.
Lovers whisper secrets on sworn stone.

Her rose is delicate and lightly dresses
His crimson nosegay, pressed to adorn stone.

The wombs of priestesses are traded here
By priests who finger prayers in the worn stone.

A flower-bearing maid makes princes' beds
Where gods are consummated, and born stone.

Her hair is bound. Her cheekbone presses down.
The royal axe licks right to the shorn stone.

Volcán de Fuego

You can walk to the top of a higher volcano,
Mexico's so-called fire volcano.

From a wonderful literary terrace, you can
Easily regard the admired volcano

And return to a D-day where warriors ruled
An ayate-and-ruby attired volcano.

Varied in texture, hue and sheen –
From base to summit, it's an inspired volcano.

For a digital fantasy cinema movie,
You'll need franchising rights to the entire volcano –

And to all its surrounds, so your dragons can languish
in the core of this blackrock spired volcano.

Here darkness and hellfire in fury blast forth
From this purebred Tarascan-sired volcano.

In these verdant and unexplored forests and valleys,
It could easily be the chief's pyre volcano

That artists, with sweetrock volcanic oils,
Might paint: as a Levantine briar volcano –

Or as the dawn sun touching on eastern New Zealand's
Long extinct tweed shire volcano –

Or as a sunset beach, looking up from Kihei
To the light of an evening's expired volcano –

Or as khaki spring water, gushing out through the sulphur,
Since Bok-ke's a smallish mired volcano.

Yes, upon our arrival in La Fortuna we were
Aliens ascending a now-tired volcano:

A bitchy secretary and a posthumous chorus
For their live-cam event at their hired volcano.

A Short History of the Ghazal

Ever since the ghazal was introduced into English poetry, there has been confusion as to what constitutes a ghazal and which poems have a right to be identified as ghazals in English. By tracing the history and development of the ghazal over the more than a millennia and a half that it has been in existence, this article seeks to put recent efforts into perspective. It is hoped that a better understanding of the diverse and changing nature of ghazal writing in the past will help us to envision how the rich variety of contemporary works being written in English today fit into the broader context of ghazal writing.

This article traces the evolution of the ghazal. Starting with the ghazal's origins in the pre-Islamic Arabian *qasīdah*, it follows the ghazal's development in Medieval Arabia and Persia, and its adoption into the literatures of other languages and cultures.

Origins of the Ghazal

In pre-Islamic Arabia, the ghazal was not recognized as a major genre of poetry. This was the era of the "golden odes" – the great Arabic *qasīdahs*. There were various genres for the *qasīdah*, including the panegyric (*madīh*), the moralizing poem (*hikam*), the lampoon (*hijā'*), and the boast (*fakhr*). However, the ghazal – the love poem – was not one of these.

Instead, what was later to become the ghazal was an integral part of nearly every pre-Islamic grand *qasīdah*. These *qasīdahs* were divided into three broad sections: the *nasīb*, the *rahīl*, and then whichever of the recognized poetic genres the poet intended. It is the *nasīb*, that opened the *qasīdah*, which would later develop into the ghazal.

Ibn Qutaybah (d. 889) explains, rather nostalgically, the way in which the old odes were constructed:

> I have heard some literary personalities mention that the *qasīdah* would have to begin with mention of the homeland, one's abode, and what has passed. The poet would mourn and pine about these things, address his land, and call for his

travelling companions to stop. He would do this to as a means to make mention of those who had once lived there... Then he would bring this to the *nasīb*, where he would lament the severity of his passion, the pain of separation, his longing, and his ardent love for his beloved. The purpose of this was to draw the hearts and attentions of his listeners to him, to prepare them to listen to him attentively. This is because rhapsodising about women is something close to the hearts and affections of men, since God has placed in the natural makeup of His male servants a love of dalliance (*ghazal*) and the society of women. Rarely is a man free from some manner of attachment and some real involvement – whether it be lawful or sinful.

When the poet is satisfied that he has his audience listening attentively, he follows this advantage and asserts his rights upon the listener, and thereby brings the *rahīl* where he laments the fatigue of travel, the passing of sleepless nights, the oppressiveness of the midday heat, and the emaciation of his camel.

Once he is sure he has justified to his listener his hope (of recompense), he starts with the praises (*madīh*), encouraging his listener's generosity and patronage, asserting the superiority of his grace over that of his peers, and how incomparable it still is to his lofty stature.

A praiseworthy poet is one who employs this style, giving equal weight to each of the sections, not allowing any section of the poem to dominate over the others. He does not prolong anything too much so as to bore the audience, nor does he abbreviate anything so much as to leave the people wanting to hear more.[1]

Though Ibn Qutaybah gives the panegyric poem as his example for the *qasīdah*'s final section, it does not have to be in that genre. The *qasīdah* could be in any of the other recognized poetic genres.

Ibn Qutaybah is credited with being the first literary thinker to attempt to explain the purpose behind beginning the *qasīdah* with the *nasīb*.[2] His opinion was that the *nasīb* was essentially a means for the poet to win over the attention of his audience. This would remain the predominant view on the matter throughout the Middle Ages.

An alternate view suggested by Ibn Rashīq al-Qayrawānī (d. 1064?) is that the amorous introduction was a means of bringing the poet into the proper poetic mindset. He draws this conclusion from the following personal account of the Ummayad-era poet Dhū al-Rummah (696-735), which he relates as follows:

> Dhū al-Rummah was asked: "What do you do as a poet when you have writer's block?"
>
> He replied: "How can I ever have writer's block when I possess the keys to unlock my poetry?"
>
> He was told: "Well, those are what we are asking you about."
>
> He said: "They are: solitude, and thinking about my loved ones."[3]

Ibn Rashīq then comments: "This is because of his longing. Indeed, when a poet begins his *qasīdah* with the *nasīb*, he has placed his foot in the stirrup."[4]

The contemporary scholar Hayāt Jāsim regards the *nasīb* as having fulfilled an important psychological need both for the poet and the audience within the context of Bedouin life. She writes:

> Love, being as it is an emotion of beauty, is intrinsically tied to the hopes of all people. They pine for it in youth, take pleasure in it during maturity, and lament its loss in old age. Love is a glimmer of light at times of despair, a wave of strength in times of weakness, and a trusty weapon against severity and hardship. Why would the pre-Islamic poets not exploit this emotion as a foil against the harsh and austere realities of their way of life, where the threat of death was always present? Love served to represent what was good in life. Love culminating in union represented happiness and prosperity. Separation and tears represented bittersweet pain and sweet sorrow.[5]

Essentially, for a people whose lifestyle was one of violence, hardship, and material want, the various manifestations of love were the most precious and valued possibilities of worldly delight.

Recent scholarship attempts to trace the *nasīb* further back in time, back to its origins in prehistory. Scholars like Suzanne Pinckney Stetkevych and Jaroslav Stetkevych do not accept the idea that the pre-Islamic *nasīb* was merely a rhetorical prelude or a concrete representation of Bedouin life. Jaroslav Stetkevych, by analysing the recurrent motifs in the *nasīb*, identifies its origin in Ancient Near Eastern ritual, myth, and poetry.[6]

Suzanne Pinckney Stetkevych argues that the three parts of the classical Arabic *qasīdah* owe their origins to the poetics of ritual of the Ancient Near East, formulated on a seasonal pattern. She writes on the panegyric *qasīdah*:

> (W)e are dealing with a Bedouin variant of the Ancient Middle Eastern agrarian pattern in which the "harvest" is not the seasonally determined one of grain, but the metaphorical "harvest" of human lives on the battle "field."[7]

In this, she follows the model presented by Theodor Gaster, who describes the structure of Ancient Near Eastern seasonal ritual as having been comprised of two rites of Emptying followed by two rites of Filling. These four rites in order were: mortification – purgation – invigoration – and jubilation.

The rite of mortification, in agrarian societies, symbolized the state of "suspended animation" at the end of the year when the annual lease on life had drawn to a close and the new one had not yet begun. The rite of purgation symbolized the agrarian community's attempt to rid itself of all the physical and moral evil that might threaten the renewal of its vitality in the coming year. The rite of invigoration was the community's attempt to procure a new lease on life. Finally, the rite of jubilation represented the sense of relief at the commencement of the new year and the continuation of the natural cycle.

Stetkevych argues that the *nasīb*, the *rahīl*, and the *madīh* originated in these four rites. She explains:

> ... Ibn Qutaybah's formulation is tripartite. It is quite possible, however, to see in the *nasīb*, which comprises a description of the abandoned encampment, the lost mistress, the complaint against old age, etc., an expression of mortification, "suspended animation"; in the *rahīl* which comprises the recounting of the hardships of the desert crossing and the description of the poet's mount, the she-camel, purgation; the third and final section, in this case *madīh* (panegyric), must then be understood as encompassing both aspects of Filling, invigoration and jubilation, as such common elements as the battle or hunt followed by the feast would certainly allow.⁸

Research into the origins of the *nasīb* – and by extension the ghazal which it would later become – is certainly intriguing. There can be no doubt that the fully-formed pre-Islamic *qasīdah* that we see at the dawn of Arabic written literature did not suddenly appear out of nowhere. It had behind it a long, unrecorded history that can only be deduced through indirect means.

The Flowering of the Arabian Ghazal

During the early Islamic era (622-661), there were no substantial changes in poetic practice. The pre-Islamic tradition continued more or less as it was, except that the writing of shorter poems became more popular, often for political and religious purposes. However, the ghazal was not given any particularly special attention among these shorter works.⁹

The ghazal came into its own as a poetic genre during the Ummayyad Era (661-750) and continued to flower and develop in the early Abbasid Era (750-861).

Though three-part *qasīdahs* continued to be written, it was during Ummayyad times that the pre-Islamic *qasīdah* was broken up into its constituent parts. Lampoons, boasts, panegyric poems, and moralizing poems were now written on their own. Even the term *qasīdah* started to become more or less synonymous with the more general notion of a "formal poem".

The ghazal was also separated out during this time, becoming a stand-alone poetic genre in its own right, and as such it enjoyed exceptional popularity and considerable patronage.

The ghazal, along with the other Arabic poetic genres, inherited from its pre-Islamic origins the formal verse structure of the *qasīdah*. A poem in this form is always constructed from lines of a single meter, where each line (called a *bayt* in Arabic and a *sher* in Persian) is constructed from two metrical hemistiches and ends on the same rhyme (*qāfiyah*). The Persians would later add certain other features to the ghazal, as we shall see, but the underlying form would remain the same.

Though the ghazal during the Ummayad period was understood to be a poetic genre dealing with the theme of longing for the beloved, it also had to adhere strictly to the formal verse structure it inherited from the *qasīdah*. The marriage between this particular verse form and the theme of longing would continue to be the defining character of the ghazal wherever it was adopted in the world. Even when formal innovations and variations were introduced into the ghazal by practitioners of the art in the contexts of different languages and cultures, the theme of longing – whether it be romantic, erotic, mystical, or divine – and this underlying form would always be there.

As the ghazal came into its own during the Ummayad period, it grew into the most popular poetic genre of the time, and would remain so for centuries to come. The middle and upper classes of the new and growing urban centres of the Arab world demanded entertainment, and at the forefront of this new entertainment industry were music and song. The popularity of the ghazal reached dizzying heights due to its suitability for musical diversions.

The nature of the ghazal changed drastically to meet the demands of light musical entertainment. It generally became a briefer composition. Its choice of meter changed. Instead of the long, ponderous meters that had been favoured for the *qasīdahs* –

meters like *kāmil, basīt,* and *rajaz* – lighter meters like *khafīf, ramal,* and *muqtarab* were preferred, along with abridged variants of the longer meters.¹⁰ Topically, instead of focusing on nostalgic reminisces of the homeland and the loved-ones left behind, the focus of ghazals became romantic or erotic, or otherwise highly stylised and affected.¹¹

As the popularity of the ghazal grew, different schools of ghazal writing developed, which introduced into Arabic literature a rich variety of poetic sub-genres. The most important of these sub-genres were as follows:

1. Courtly Love (`udharī). This genre of poetry focuses on devotion towards a woman who is beyond approach and with whom love can never be consummated.¹² Poems written in this genre focus on the pain of longing and the passions of the heart and are nearly free of eroticism and references to physical desire.

Poets writing in this genre usually devote all their output, or at least a long sequence of poems, to a single love interest. Jamīl b. Ma`mar (d. 701) has his Buthaynah. Kuthayyir b. `Abd al-Rahmān (660?-723?) has his `Azzah. `Urwah b. Hizām has his `Afrah. Tawbah b. al-Humayr has his Laylā.

Describing this genre of ghazal as the genre of "courtly love" is accurate insofar as the themes of these ghazals are nearly identical to those of the courtly love tradition of the European High Middle Ages. However, this genre was not exceptionally popular at the urban courts. It was rather a favourite of the desert regions of the Hijaz and Najd.

2. Erotic (*hissī*). Representing the genre most popular with the Umayyad urban elite, the erotic ghazal is typified by graphic physical descriptions of the object of desire, often limb by limb. `Umar b.Abī Rabī`ah (644- 712/719) is the most notable poet of erotic ghazals.

3. Introductory (*tamhīdī*). This genre of ghazal, also referred to as "traditional" (*taqlīdī*) is specifically employed to act as a prologue or introduction to poems of other genres. This practice is a holdover from the pre-Islamic three-part *qasīdah*. There are two differences between this form and the *nasīb* of the three-part *qasīdah*. First, the introductory ghazal is highly stylised, and second, it enters straight into the main genre of the poem without being followed by a *rahīl*. This genre was perfected by Jarīr (650-728), Farazdaq (641-728/730), and al-Akhtal (640-710).

The practice of beginning poems of other genres with a ghazal went in and out of vogue more than once, and at various times had its ardent supporters and equally ardent detractors. This was particularly the case during the early Abbasid period.[13]

It was within this genre that a certain literary art was perfected – that is the art of *husn al-takhallus* (literally: beautiful extrication), the art of modulating smoothly from one genre to another within a poem. During the pre-Islamic period, the *nasīb* could end rather abruptly into the *rahīl*, a practice which was frowned upon for the introductory ghazal of the Ummayad period.

The introductory ghazal developed a further sub-genre of its own: the conceit (*qaydī*). This is where the ghazal itself is an elaborate ruse for the main genre of the poem, which would quite often be a lampoon. Ibn Qays al-Ruqayyāt (d. 704) is known for this sub-genre. Taha Hussein credits him as its originator.[14]

4. Homoerotic (*mudhakkar*). This genre of the ghazal became important in the early Abbasid period. One of its most renowned practitioners was Abū al-Nuwās (750-810).

The Spread of the Arabian Ghazal

The ghazal spread from Arabia into Africa and Spain, as well as into Persia. In medieval Spain, ghazals were written in Hebrew as well as Arabic. An important writer of Hebrew ghazals, and one of its chief defenders, was Moses ibn Ezra (1058-1155).[15] There is a remote possibility that ghazals were also written in Mozarabic (an early form of Spanish written in Arabic script) since *jarchas*, poems related to the *muwashshah* – a particularly Andalusian Arabic poetic form – have been found in this language.

Poems in the Arabic form have been written in a number of major West African literary languages like Hausa and Fulfulde. African practitioners of this type of poetry were as concerned with adapting the Arabic meters as they were with emulating the themes and formal structure of Arabic poetry. Hausa poets, for instance, adopted the Arabic forms and meters into their written poetry in the nineteenth century.[16] In doing so, they had to translate the Arabic quantitative metrical sequences into roughly corresponding sequences based on the heavy and light syllables of the Hausa language.

The ghazal was also adopted very early on by the Persians, who developed it into something uniquely their own. These developments will be discussed at length in the following section.

Wherever the Arabian ghazal was introduced into the literature of another language – whether we are talking about Africa, Spain, or Persia – it was preceded by the cultural dominance of the Arabic language in that region. Arabic was, at the very least, a major language of education in those cultures at the time when the ghazal was first adopted as a local poetic form. The poets who pioneered the introduction of ghazals in their native languages had all written ghazals in Arabic as well.

The Evolution of the Persian Ghazal

The Persians during the Abbasid period were keen on adopting Arabic verse structures and meters into the Persian language. The beginnings of the ghazal in Persian was a time of imitating and adapting the Arabic form.

In truth, the earliest ghazals written in Persian are essentially Arabian ghazals. Only two real differences can be discerned in these poems that we might call "Arabo-Persian". The first is a change in sensibilities regarding the poetic line. The early Persian ghazal poets did not exhibit radical enjambment between the hemistiches, nor did they generally employ any kind of enjambment between the lines, which were showing themselves to be more and more like couplets, and less like individual long lines. There was, like in the Arabic ghazals, a strong overall continuity and flow of meaning between the lines of the poem. The poems were still an organic whole. This would gradually change over time, with the couplets growing more and more autonomous.

The second difference between the early ghazals written in Persian and their Arabic counterparts concerns the use of *tasrī`* (in Persian ghazals: *matla*), which is to have the first line/couplet of the poem employ the rhyme in both of its hemistiches. In the early Persian ghazals, this practice becomes a formal norm instead of an optional embellishment.

It should come as no surprise that Persian poets emulated other genres of Arabic poetry as well. They also wrote panegyric poems, lampoons, boasts, and didactic compositions after the Arabic models. Browne classifies Persian poetry into two broad categories: "many-rhymed" where the two hemistiches of a single line rhyme with each other, but with the poem exhibiting a variety of rhymes throughout, and "one-rhymed" where a single rhyme is kept throughout the poem and the only place where the first hemistich rhymes is in the opening line/couplet.[17] The former is represented by the uniquely Persian *mathnawi*, while the latter include the borrowed Arabic forms – the *qasīdah*, the *qit`ah*, and the ghazal – as well as some hybrid inventions like the *ruba`iyyat*.

What distinguishes the ghazal during this early period is the ghazal's focus and textual style. Mūsā explains: "The style of the ghazal required a sweetness of word choice and a smoothness of meaning. The meters chosen for the ghazal were to be the most musical ones, like *hazaj*, *ramal*, *mudāri`*, and *khafīf*, though there was no formal prohibition against the use of other metres."[18]

It is interesting to note that many of these are the same light meters that the Arab poets had already begun favouring for their ghazals during the Ummayad period.

Also, Persian ghazals usually tended to be brief, usually between seven to fifteen couplets – though there are a number of important exceptions to this – while Arabic ghazals, as well as Persian *qasīdahs*, could be much longer.

Since the above description of the ghazals written in Persian at this time can apply to quite a number of Arabic ghazals and none of the differences constitute an actual formal deviation from the Arabic norm, we can say that these earliest Persian examples still fit into the broad formal pattern of the Arabian ghazal.

An important Persian writer of ghazals at this time was Abdullah Jafar Rudaki (859-941). Dr. Reza Zadeh Shafegh counts him as "the first of the great poets of Iran".[19]

Rudaki was certainly the most praised of the ghazal writers of his time. Al-Unsuri praised his ghazals. Abu al-Fadl al-Bal`ami said: "There is no one among the Arabs or the non-Arabs like Rudaki."[20] This statement is telling. It shows the close proximity that existed at the time between Persian and Arabic literature, in that critics would readily compare between the two.

Development of the 'Early Persian' Form

As time went on, the Persian ghazal grew into a unique poetic form. While the topics that could be addressed by the ghazal widened – though still remaining within the general theme of longing – its form grew more and more distinctive.

The first significant development that occurred in the form of the Persian ghazal was the adoption of the *takhallus*. This is the practice of mentioning the poet's pen name in the final couplet.

This *takhallus* should not be confused with the disengagement of the Arabian introductory ghazal. It is unlikely that the term even derives from the *husn al-takhallus* of the Arabian introductory ghazal. It is more likely that this use of the term is derived from an Arabic notational mark called the *takhallus*, which used to be written above a word in a document to identify it as the author's name. The *takhallus* of the Persian ghazal is a Persian innovation, and it is a clear formal addition to the essential Arabic form.[21]

Like any other stylistic trend in literature, it is difficult to pinpoint exactly when the *takhallus* came into vogue. It was not at all in evidence during the era of Rudaki.[22] However, by the twelfth century, Musa asserts that "poets were consistent in mentioning the *takhallus* and they rarely neglected it thereafter."[23]

By contrast, Browne does not regard the *takhallus* as being a standard fixture of the Persian ghazal "before the Mongol invasion"[24] which took place in the year 1218.

Yahya Dawud `Abbas identifies this innovation with the poet Sina'i (d. 1141), a third of whose poems end with his *takhallus*.[25] He also points out that Jalal al-Din al-Asfahani (d. 1192) never used the *takhallus*. Al-Khaqani and al-Anwari were consistent in their use of the *takhallus*.

The adoption of the *takhallus* was most likely a gradual development, becoming more and more ubiquitous throughout the 12th century. By the time of Muslih-ul-Din Saadi (1184-1283/1291?), it had become the formal norm.[26]

This development was coupled with another growing trend towards a far greater degree of autonomy to the meaning of each couplet. This is another marked departure from the ghazal's Arabic forebears.

These two qualities, therefore, typify the ghazals written in Persian through the remainder of Ghaznavid era (which lasted until 1187) up to sometime after the Mongol invasion.

We can call this form, typical of the 12th and early 13th centuries, the "early Persian ghazal". It is a form typified by brevity, *takhallus*, and a substantial autonomy of the couplet. It is already quite distinct formally from its Arabic counterpart, as well as from the Persian *qasīdah* and *qit`ah*, the other Arabic-derived forms.

Saadi was one of the most important writers of this form of ghazal. He lived at the very end of the period in question, and indeed, had to flee from the Mongols when they invaded his home city of Shiraz in the year 1264.[27] He is regarded by many to be one of the greatest Persian ghazal writers of all time, comparable to no less than Hafiz.

Development of the 'Late Persian' Form

Persian ghazals evolved substantially after the Mongol invasion, an era of Persian history known as the Early Mongol Period. The *radīf*, which had been a relatively rare device first introduced as a decorative embellishment, became a standard formal feature during this time. The *radīf* is the Persian refrain, a repeating word or phrase that comes immediately after the rhyme in every rhyming line of the poem. We can appreciate how important the *radīf* is as a formal innovation when we realise that it necessitates placing the rhyming word (*qāfiyah*) earlier in the metrical sequence.

In this era, the couplets remained extremely autonomous in meaning, even growing in autonomy until each couplet often behaved like a miniature poem in its own right. This is the poetic ideal where the couplet is compared to "a precious pearl in a necklace."

We can call this form the "late Persian ghazal", the final form that Persian ghazals were to take. Like the *takhallus*, it is hard to chart the development of the *radīf* as a feature of Persian ghazals with exact precision.

The *radīf* existed as a very uncommon ornament in Persian poetry from quite early on.[28] Instances of *radīf* are found in a few poems dating from before the tenth century. Rudaki exhibits *radīf* in two of his poems that are not ghazals. Other early isolated examples exist in various poetic genres for poets like Mahmud-i Varraq, Shahid-i Balkhi, Abu Shukur, Ma`rufi, and Daqiqi. These are the very first known examples of the *radīf* in post-Islamic Persian verse.[29] At this time, however, the *radīf* is a rare ornament that could hardly be said to have any particular affiliation with the ghazal.

By the twelfth century, the *radīf* had become a common poetic ornament in Persian poetry in general, though still not a strict formal convention of the ghazal. Franklin D. Lewis cites the following description of the *radīf* from Rashid al-Din Vatvat's twelfth century treatise on poetics:

> The *radīf* is a word, or more than a word, in Persian poetry which recurs [in each line] after the rhyming word. Such poetry is called by practitioners of the craft *muraddaf* – poetry with a refrain. The Arabs do not use refrains, except in the case of recent innovators attempting to display their virtuosity. Most Persian poems have a refrain, for the expertise and versatility of the poet is made obvious in composing poems with a refrain.[30]

Lewis then comments that by the time of the poet Farid al-Din `Attar (d. 1221?) the *radīf* had become as commonplace as Rashid al-Din describes it to be, with over half of the poems in Attar's *Divan* having a *radīf* after its rhyme.[31]

A few of Saadi's ghazals are written with *radīf*. By contrast, the *radīf* is the norm for the ghazals of his younger contemporary, Jalal al-Din Rumi (1207-1273), who is only a little more than twenty years his junior. This can be seen in Rumi's exquisite *Divan-e Shams*.

The *radīf* becomes the overwhelming norm for the ghazals of the later Persian masters, like the fourteenth-century Hafiz, though most of the later poets occasionally wrote ghazals in the older style without *radīf*.

It is important to keep in mind that even though the *takhallus* and *radīf* had become important formal elements of the Persian ghazal, they were not taken as necessary elements for a poem to be recognized as a ghazal. Either or both features could be – and sometimes were – dispensed with.

The essential characteristics defining a ghazal remained what they had always been: formally, a specific type of metrical construction (*bayt/sher*) with monorhyme (*qāfiyah*), and thematically, the topic of longing for some object of desire. Therefore, what really separates the Persian ghazal from its Arabian and Arabo-Persian antecedents is the Persian ghazal's distinctive linear autonomy.

During the thirteenth century, the ghazal took a pre-eminent place in Persian poetry, due to the growth of Sufism.[32] The ghazal's theme of longing proved particularly well suited to Persian mysticism, and from this time onward, the ghazal becomes less a vehicle for romantic or erotic love – as it would remain for many Arabic ghazals – and more a form devoted to the expression of the spiritual longing to connect with the Divine.

The development of the Persian ghazal from its Arabo-Persian beginnings through the early Persian form to the late Persian form cannot be dated with any precision, due to the fluidity of the process and the overlapping of the various developmental trends. At the same time, the prevalence of different formal conventions in different eras provides us with a clear developmental progression over the course of centuries culminating in the Persian ghazal settling down into its distinctive form, possessing *takhallus*, *radīf*, and extreme linear autonomy, by the end of the thirteenth century.

The Spread of the Persian Ghazal

The late Persian form of the ghazal spread out from Persian-speaking areas, first into the Indian subcontinent and the Turkish regions of Asia, and then into Europe.

In the case of the Turkish and Indian ghazals, poets who were conversant in Persian were the ones to adopt the ghazal into their native tongues. The Persian language was at the time the dominant literary language in Central Asia and India, and most of the ghazal writers who wrote in other languages also had Persian ghazals to their credit. This is similar to how the ghazal first spread from Arabia into Persia, Africa, and Spain.

An important Ottoman Turkish ghazal writer was Fuzuli (1483-1556), who wrote in Azerbaijani Turkish. Another Turkish master was the Afghani poet Ali-Shir Nava'i (1441-1501), who wrote in the now extinct Chagatai language, and as such is regarded as the founder of Uzbek literature. He is also referred to as the "Chaucer of the Turks", due to the important role he played in establishing the literary prestige of the Turkic languages.

In India, ghazals of the late Persian form were written in Persian as well as a number of Indian languages. Amir Khusru (1253-1325) was one of the earlier Indian poets writing in this form, and he wrote ghazals in both Persian and Hindi. Ghalib (1796-1869) was a one of the most renowned practitioners of this form in Urdu.

Today, ghazals in the late Persian form are written in Hindi, Gugurati, Punjabi, Bengali and every other major language of the Indian subcontinent.

The ghazal was introduced into Europe in the 19th century through translations of Persian works. Goethe's translations of ghazals – as well as his famous collection of oriental-influenced poems entitled the *West-Eastern Divan* – inspired other German poets, including Friedrich Rückert (1788-1866) and August Graf von

Platen (1796-1835) to go farther and write in the ghazal form itself, which, since the nineteenth century, has developed into a substantial body of German poetry.

Among the most important of these works are August von Platen's anthologies *Ghaselen* (1821) and *Neue Ghaselen* (1823). In the following, Ghazal 3, we can see how von Platen shows strict adherence to the late Persian form, including the employment of monorhyme – here on the sound "and" – and the *radīf* – which in this case is the word "*mich*":

Wohl mir, es heilte die liebende Hand mich,
Die mit balsamischem Blatte verband mich;
Als mich in Flammen umdrohte Verzweiflung,
Deckte des Glaubens asbesten Gewand mich;
Irrend durchstrich ich das waldige Dickicht,
Doch Philomele, die zärtliche, fand mich;
Sterbend im Ozean schwamm ich, der Delphin
Segelte ruhig ans blumige Land mich;
Schlüpfrigen Höhen entglitt ich zum Abgrund,
Aber die Rebe des Berges umwand mich.

An important convention seen here, and one that has persisted in ghazal writing for languages using the Roman alphabet, is to break the *bayt/sher* into two lines at the hemistich. We should also note that these are not separated by von Platen into distinct couplets. The stanzaic form would develop later on and become a convention for ghazals written in English.

Agha Sahid Ali (1942-2001) is widely regarded as the leading proponent of the late Persian form in English. He promotes this form in his own ghazal writing and through the landmark anthology he edited in 2000 entitled *Ravishing DisUnities: Real Ghazals in English*.

The Story is Not Over Yet

Recent developments in the ghazal writing of the Indian subcontinent include a relaxation of certain formal restrictions. According to Abhay Avachat, many contemporary Urdu ghazals use alternating meters for each hemistich of the *sher* and many poems dispense with the *takhallus* while retaining the *radīf*.[33]

Numerous innovations have taken place as a consequence of the ghazal being adopted by poets writing in European languages. Western cultures, the English-speaking ones no less than the others, tend to adopt, adapt, and modify various artistic forms from other cultures to their own needs at a rapid pace, and this is certainly true for the ghazal. From the onset of ghazal writing in German in the nineteenth century, European writers have used the conventional meters of their own languages, rather than trying to emulate the meters of the people from whom they borrowed the ghazal form. Few attempts have been made to adapt the Arabic meters and rhythms into European languages, which is in stark contrast to what had been the case when the Persian and African poets first adopted the Arabian form into their own languages.

Many contemporary ghazals, moreover, are written in free verse. However, keeping in harmony with the overall ghazal form, there is a tendency in free-verse ghazals to exhibit a degree of internal consistency regarding line length. It is also very common for English ghazals to have *radīf* and no rhyme, a situation that had never appeared before the twentieth century. Indeed, many ghazals written in English possess only two distinctive features – the couplet form and the autonomy of the couplet. It would seem that the autonomy of the *sher* in the Persian ghazal is what attracts many English-language poets to the form.

This is undoubtedly the case with Adrienne Rich, who after working on a translation project of Ghalib's ghazals, composed ghazals of her own authorship in free-verse couplets. These include two sequences: *Homage to Ghalib* in 1968 – described by David Caplan as "the ghazal sequence that would be the first published by an American poet"[34] – and *The Blue Ghazals*. She says the following about her reason for writing ghazals:

49

> I certainly had to find an equivalent for the kinds of fragmentation I was feeling, and confusion. One thing that was very helpful to me was working on the translations from the Urdu poet Mirzah Ghalib, which led me to write original ghazals. There, I found a structure which allowed for a highly associative field of images. And once I saw how that worked, I felt instinctively, this is exactly what I need, there is no traditional Western order that I have found that will contain all these materials.[35]

The same tendencies can be found in the ghazals of John Thompson's 1978 *Stilt Jack*, published posthumously. Dan Reve asserts that Thompson (1938–1976) "is to be credited with the introduction and dissemination of the ghazal in Canada."[36] Thompson proved influential on other Canadian poets, particularly Phyllis Webb and Douglas Barbour.

One interesting and recent formal development in English ghazal writing is what we might call the "tercet ghazal", a form developed by Robert Bly for his anthology *The Night Abraham Called to the Stars*. This form can be described as a poem constructed from a series of autonomous tercets, each tercet consisting of highly enjambed free-verse lines of relatively uniform length. In its fullest realization, the final line of the tercet ends upon the *radīf*, which introduces itself at the end of the first tercet's initial line. All the poems in the anthology are composed of exactly six tercets. Many do not employ *radīf* at the end of each tercet. However, some, like the title poem, repeat a word throughout the tercets, which then concludes the poem.

Is the Ghazal a Form or a Genre?

Another important twentieth century trend in ghazal writing – especially for European languages, but true also for Asian languages – is to focus on the ghazal as a form to the exclusion of its being a genre. Ghazals are frequently being defined purely by some or all of their conspicuous formal elements – monorhyme, *sher*/couplet arrangement, *takhallus*, *radīf*, and the autonomy of the *sher*/couplet – and not by the theme of longing. The formal aspects of the ghazal are being applied to poems of every conceivable topic – even to Language poems.

In Asia, this is a more striking and radical development than Western poets might appreciate it to be. In the Persian, Turkish, and South Asian literary cultures of the past, a poem written with *radīf*, linear autonomy, and *takhallus*, brought with it an expectation of a literary treatment of longing – whether sensual or spiritual – a poem that would focus on the "beloved" in one way or another. This is still primarily the case in Asia. However, it is no longer difficult to find the formal norms of the ghazal being used to treat a wide range of other quite disparate topics and themes.

This divorce between form and theme – dissolving a marriage that had persisted worldwide in ghazal writing for over 1300 years – has also taken place in the Arab world, but in the opposite way. This has resulted from the introduction of free verse into Arabic poetry in the mid-twentieth century, which precipitated a revolution in how literary terms are defined. The term *qasīdah* – which has always before indicated a poem with strict meter and rhyme – is now being used for free verse poems as well. In modern Arabic usage, the word *qasīdah* is merely a generic term for "poem", so much so that in order to specify that a modern poem is written in a classical meter, it has to be qualified as "*shi´r ´amūdī*" or a "formal" poem.

This has had many far-reaching consequences for Arabic poetic discourse. For one thing, it has resulted in a change in how the word "ghazal" is defined. In modern Arabic literature, "ghazal" has become purely a genre term, and not a term defining both form and genre. In the past, a poem about love or longing, if it was written in any other verse form besides that of the *qasīdah*, would not be referred to as a ghazal. If its form were that of a *nazam* or a *maqām*, it would not be regarded as a proper poem. If a love poem were written as a *muwashshah*, it would deserve respect as a poem – but would generally be referred to as a *muwashshah* on the theme of love.

By contrast, in contemporary Arabic discourse, the term "ghazal" is purely thematic. A poem written in free verse that deals with the themes of love or longing is called a ghazal, regardless of its form. This explains why a free verse poet like Nizār Qabbānī (1923-1998) can be lauded in the Arab world as one of the twentieth century's foremost ghazal writers, and why recent anthologies of ghazals in Arabic will have free verse and prose poems presented alongside those written in the classical form. This development in the Arabic usage of the word "ghazal" is not likely to have an impact on how the term is understood by speakers of other languages. As a genre term simply meaning "love poem", it is something that speakers of other languages can dispense with. The opposite trend, to use "ghazal" as a purely formal term, seems now to be well-established in English poetic discourse – though exactly how that form is to be defined has remained a point of contention.

---

[1] al-Daynūrī, Ibn Qutaybah. *al-Shi`r wa al-Shu`arā'* (Poetry and Poets). al-Warrāq. (vol.1, p.5).

[2] al-Muqbil, Badr b. `Alī. *Shi`r al-Ghazal fī Daw' Manhaj al-Adab al-Islāmī* (Ghazal Poetry in Light of an Islamic Approach to Literature) Dammam: Dār Ibn al-Jawzī. 2007. (p. 350).

[3] al-Qayrawānī, Ibn Rashīq. *al-`Umdah fī Mahāsin al-Shi`r wa Adabihi wa Naqdihi* (A Sourcebook on the Qualities, Refinements, and Criticism of Poetry) ed. Muhammad Muhyī al-Dīn `Abd al-Hamīd. Beirut: Dār al-Jīl. 1981. (vol. 1 p. 206).

[4] *ibid.*

[5] Jāsim, Hayāt. *Wahdah al-Qasīdah fī al-Shi`r al-`Arabi hattā Nihāyah al-`Asr al-`Abbāsī* (The Unity of the Arabic Qasīdah up to the End of the Abbasid Period). Riyadh: Dār al-`Ulūm. 1986.

[6] Stetkevych, Jaroslav. "Toward an Arabic Elegiac Lexicon" in *Reorientations/ Arabic and Persian Poetry*. Edited by Suzanne Pinckney Stetkevych. Bloomington and Indianapolis: Indiana University Press. 1994. (p. 58).

[7] Stetkevych, Suzanne Pinckney. "Pre-Islamic Panegyric and the Poetics of Redemtion" in Reorientations/ Arabic and Persian Poetry. Edited by Suzanne Pinckney Stetkevych. Bloomington and Indianapolis: Indiana University Press. 1994. (p. 5).

[8] *ibid.* (pp. 6-7).

[9] al-Muqbil. (p. 20).

[10] Dayf, Shawqī. *Tārīkh al-Adab al-Islāmī: 2 - al-`Asr al-Islāmī* (A History of Arab Literature: 2- The Islamic Era). Cairo: Dār al-Ma`ārif. 1963. (pp. 347-348).

[11] *ibid.* (p. 348).
[12] Hussein, Taha. *Hadīth al-Arbi`ā'* (Wednesday Lectures). Egypt: Dar al-Ma`ārif. 1961. (vol. 2 pp. 15-17).
[13] al-Muqbil. (p. 346).
[14] Hussein. (vol.1, p. 252)
[15] Brann, Ross, "The Dissembling Poet in Medieval Hebrew Literature: The Dimensions of a Literary Topos" *Journal of the American Oriental Society*, Vol. 107, No. 1. (Jan. - Mar., 1987). (pp. 39-54).
[16] Schuh, Russel G. "Text and Performance in Hausa Metrics" a UCLA Occasional Paper. 1994. (pp. 1-2).
[17] Browne, Edward G. *A Literary History of Persia*. New Delhi: Goodword Books. 2002. (vol. 2 p. 25).
[18] Mūsā, Muna `Abd al-Fattāh Ahmad. *Awzān al-Shi`r al-Fārisī wa Anmātihi Hattā Nihāyah al-`Asr al-Ghaznawī* (The Meters and Forms of Persian Poetry until the End of the Ghaznavid Era) unpublished Master's thesis. Cairo: `Ayn al-Shams University. 1986. (p. 164).
[19] Shafegh, Reza Zadeh. *Tārīkh al-Adab al-Fārisī* (The History of Persian Literature –translated from the Persian into Arabic by Muhammad Mūsā Hindāwī) Dār al-Fikr al-`Arabī 1947. (p. 28).
[20] *ibid.*
[21] Hasan, Laylā Fu`ād Muhammad. *Tatawwur Fann al-Ghazal fī al-Shi`r al-Safawī* (The Evolution of the Art of the Ghazal in Safavid Poetry) unpublished PhD dissertation. Cairo: `Ayn al-Shams University. 1986. (p. 2).
[22] Mūsā. (p. 167).
[23] *ibid.* (p. 163).
[24] Browne. (vol. 2, p. 27)
[25] Hasan. (p. 3)
[26] *ibid.*
[27] Mūsā. (p. 286).
[28] Lewis, Franklin D. "The Rise and Fall of a Persian Refrain" in *Reorientations/ Arabic and Persian Poetry*. Edited by Suzanne Pinckney Stetkevych. Bloomington and Indianapolis: Indiana University Press. 1994. (p. 201) Lewis cites a possible Middle Persian origin for the practice.
[29] *ibid.* (p. 215).
[30] *ibid.* (pp. 200-201).
[31] *ibid.* (p. 201).
[32] Hasan. (p. 9).

[33] Avachat, Abhay. "What is a Ghazal?" http://smriti.com/urdu/ghazal.def.html [accessed 15 May 2007].
[34] Caplan, David. "'In That Thicket of Bitter Roots': The Ghazal in America". *The Virginia Quarterly Review*, Vol. 80, No. 4. (Fall 2004) pp. 115-134 www.vqronline.org/articles/2004/fall/caplan-that-thicket/ [accessed 15 May 2007].
[35] *ibid.*
[36] Reve, Dan. "Review of Cutting the Devil's Throat" *The Danforth Review*. http://www.danforthreview.com/reviews/poetry/steeves.html [accessed 15 May 2007].

About the Author

David Jalajel earned his PhD in Arabic from the Department of Foreign Languages at the University of the Western Cape. He is the author of *Moon Ghazals* (Beard of Bees Press, 2009), *Cthulhu on Lesbos* (Ahadada Books, 2011) -- which is a book-length poem in Sapphic stanzas -- and a chapbook in Dan Waber's *This is Visual Poetry* series (2013). His work has appeared in a diverse range of online and print journals, including *The Mayo Review, Amaze, Otoliths, Shampoo, experiential-experimental-literature, Recursive Angel, The New Post-Literate,* and *Gulf Coast*. Poems modeled after the Arabic qasida and Persian ghazal have appeared in *The Ghazal Page, Anti-, Lynx, Mizna,* and *Eclectica*.

www.ingramcontent.com/pod-product-compliance
Lightning Source LLC
Chambersburg PA
CBHW031432040426
42444CB00006B/770